This Book Belongs to

_____

And I Will Be
The Smartest Kid in the Room!

The Smartest Kid in the Room!
By Kenny 'K3' Rochon, III
and Daddy

Copyright © Perfect Publishing Co., 2020

All rights reserved. No part of this book may be reproduced mechanically, electronically, virtually, or by any other means, including photocopying without written permission of the publisher. It is illegal to copy this book, post it to any website or distribute it by any other means without permission from the publisher.

ISBN: 978-1-64810-049-9

PRINTED IN THE UNITED STATES OF AMERICA

This is dedicated my Mom and Dad and Grandpa and Grandma Ruthann Aunt Lizy, Uncle Alex, Caroline, Stephanie, Uncle Stevie, Aunt Sharron, Matt Rochon, Andrew Rochon, Aunt Jen, Uncle Patrick, Kay Kay Herwig, Brendan Herwig.

To my friend Ally, Amelia, Anthony, Barbara, Beth, Cathy, Drake, Eddie, James, Jayden, Jonah, Nico, Tyson, and all my friends at school.

And to my teacher Mrs. Kalinock.

-Kenny

This is dedicated to my favorite people in the world. My son who lights up my life and inspires me to publish a book a year for him and my loving wife who is the best mother in the world to our son. Raising a child with love is the way to ultimately bring more smiles to the world.

Also, a special thanks to Carolyn Sheltraw for her help with layout, Tara Hannon for the front cover illustration. Al Granger for his hand in making another book (almost 200) a reality and a super fun book to help fund Kenny's education.

- Ken Rochon, Jr

THE BOTTOM LINE

FACE IT, nobody owes you a living.
What you achieve, or fail to achieve in your lifetime
Is directly related to what you do or fail to do.
No one chooses his parent or childhood,
But you can choose your own direction.
Everyone has problems and obstacles to overcome,
But that too is relative to each individual.
NOTHING IS CARVED IN STONE!
You can change anything in your life
If you want to badly enough.
Excuses are for losers! Those who take responsibility for their actions
Are the real winners in life.
Winners meet life challenges head on
Knowing there are no guarantees, and give it all they've got
And never think it's too late or too early to begin.
Time plays no favorites
And will pass whether you act or not
Take control of your LIFE
Dare to Dream and take risks.......
Compete!
If you aren't willing to work for your goals
Don't expect others to.
BELIEVE IN YOURSELF!

ANIMALS

Groups

1. Group of apes is called a shrewdness
2. Group of bears is called a sloth or sleuth
3. Group of bees is called a swarm
4. Group of buffalo is called a gang or obstinacy
5. Group of camels is called a caravan
6. Group of cats is called a clowder or glaring
7. Group of crocodiles is called a bask
8. Group of crows is called a murder
9. Group of dogs is called a pack
10. Group of elephants is called a parade
11. Group of falcons is called a cast
12. Group of fish is called a school
13. Group of frogs is called a army
14. Group of geese is called a gaggle
15. Group of giraffes is called a tower
16. Group of gorillas is called a band
17. Group of hippopotami is called a bloat
18. Group of hyenas is called a cackle
19. Group of jaguars is called a shadow
20. Group of jellyfish is called a smack
21. Group of kangaroos is called a troop or mob
22. Group of kittens is called a litter
23. Group of lemurs is called a conspiracy
24. Group of leopards is called a leap
25. Group of lions is called a pride
26. Group of monkeys is called a barrel or troop
27. Group of owls is called a parliament
28. Group of parrots is called a pandemonium
29. Group of porcupines is called a prickle
30. Group of ravens is called an unkindness
31. Group of rhinoceroses is called a crash
32. Group of sharks is called a shiver
33. Group of skunks is called a stench
34. Group of snakes is called a nest
35. Group of squirrels is called a dray or scurry
36. Group of swans is called a bevy or game
37. Group of tigers is called an ambush or streak
38. Group of turtles is called a bale or nest
39. Group of wolves is called a pack
40. Group of zebras is called a zeal

Largest
1. Largest animal is the blue whale
2. Largest land animal is the African elephant
3. Largest living bird is the Ostrich with a height of 9 feet
4. Largest land carnivore is the Brown Bear and Polar Bear reaching 10 feet tall and 1 ton
5. Largest living fish is the whale shark which is 40 feet long
6. Largest reptile is the Saltwater Crocodile growing to 17 feet
7. Tallest living animal is a Giraffe with a height of 19 feet

Mammals
1. Give birth to live babies
2. Feed their babies mother's milk
3. Have hair or fur
4. Are warm blooded
5. More developed brain
6. Move around using limbs known as tetrapods (means four limbs)

ART

1. Salvator Mundi is the most expensive painting sold in auction that sold for $450.3M
2. Leonardo DaVinci painted the Mona Lisa displayed at the Louvre in Paris, France
3. Michelangelo created most famous Statue of David located in Florence, Italy

BOY SCOUTS

A Scout is:

TRUSTWORTHY. Tell the truth and keep promises. People can depend on you.

LOYAL. Show that you care about your family, friends, Scout leaders, school, and country.

HELPFUL. Volunteer to help others without expecting a reward.

FRIENDLY. Be a friend to everyone, even people who are very different from you.

COURTEOUS. Be polite to everyone and always use good manners.

KIND. Treat others as you want to be treated. Never harm or kill any living thing without good reason.

OBEDIENT. Follow the rules of your family, school, and pack. Obey the laws of your community and country.

CHEERFUL. Look for the bright side of life. Cheerfully do tasks that come your way. Try to help others be happy.

THRIFTY. Work to pay your own way. Try not to be wasteful. Use time, food, supplies, and natural resources wisely.

BRAVE. Face difficult situations even when you feel afraid. Do what you think is right despite what others might be doing or saying.

CLEAN. Keep your body and mind fit. Help keep your home and community clean.

REVERENT. Be reverent toward God. Be faithful in your religious duties. Respect the beliefs of others.

GEOGRAPHY

"Don't tell me how educated you are, tell me how much you have travelled."
— The Prophet Mohammed

Africa

1. Home to the largest land animal is the African elephant
2. It is the 2nd largest continent on Earth
3. 1500 to 2000 languages are spoken
4. Home to the longest river in the world, the Nile River
5. Home to the University of Karueein, the oldest university in the world, 859 AD in Fez, Morocco
6. Mansa Musa, who died in 1937 the richest man in the world ever
7. The Sahara is the world's largest desert in the world

Asia

1. Most populous continent with an estimated 4.5 billion people (60% of the earth's population)
2. Home to the top two most populated countries (China with 1.3 billion and India with 1.2 billion)
3. There are 48 countries in Asia
4. China produces 45 billion pairs of chop sticks a year
5. Home to the world's highest peak, Mount Everest over 7,300 meters (23,950 feet) in the sky

FLAGS OF THE WORLD

LANDMARKS & WONDERS OF THE WORLD

1. Acropolis, Athens, Greece
2. Angkor Wat, Cambodia
3. Bagan, Myanmar, Burma
4. Burj Khalifa, Dubai
5. Chichen Itza, Mexico
6. Christ the Redeemer, Rio de Janeiro, Brazil
7. Colosseum, Italy
8. Ephesus, Turkey
9. Eiffel Tower, France
10. Forbidden City, China
11. Golden Gate Bridge, U.S.A.
12. Grand Canyon, U.S.A
13. Great Barrier Reef, Queensland, Australia
14. Great Wall, China
15. Hagia Sophia, Turkey
16. Jerusalem
17. Kyoto, Japan
18. Lake Louise, Canada
19. Machu Picchu, Peru
20. Moai, Easter Island, Chile

21. Mount Everest, Himalayas, Nepal
22. Niagara Falls, Canada
23. Northern Lights, Norway
24. Petra, Jordan
25. Pompeii, Campia, Italy
26. Pyramids of Giza, Egypt
27. Sagrada Familia, Barcelona, Spain
28. Salar de Uyuni, Bolivia
29. Schönbrunn Palace, Vienna, Austria
30. Sigiria, Sri Lanka
31. St. Basil's Cathedral, Russia
32. St. Peter's Basilica, Vatican City
33. Statue of Liberty, NY, USA
34. Stonehenge, Wiltshire, England
35. Table Mountain, Cape Town, South Africa
36. Taj Mahal, India
37. Terracotta Warriors, Xi'an, China
38. Uluru, Northern Territory, Australia
39. Venice, Italy
40. Victoria Falls, Zimbabwe

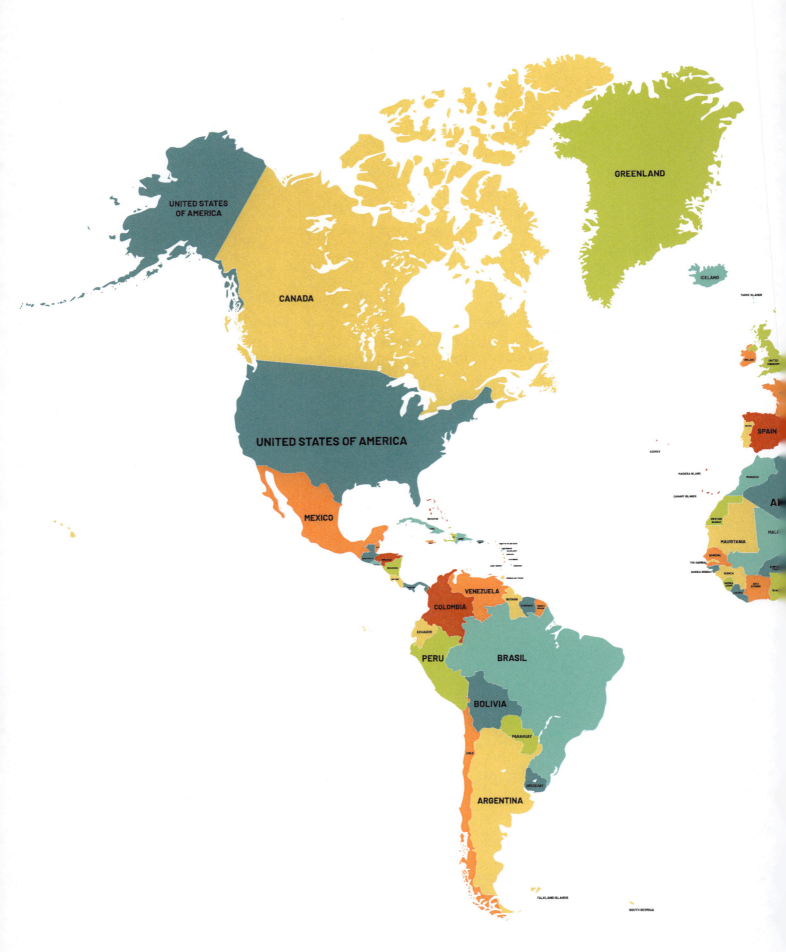

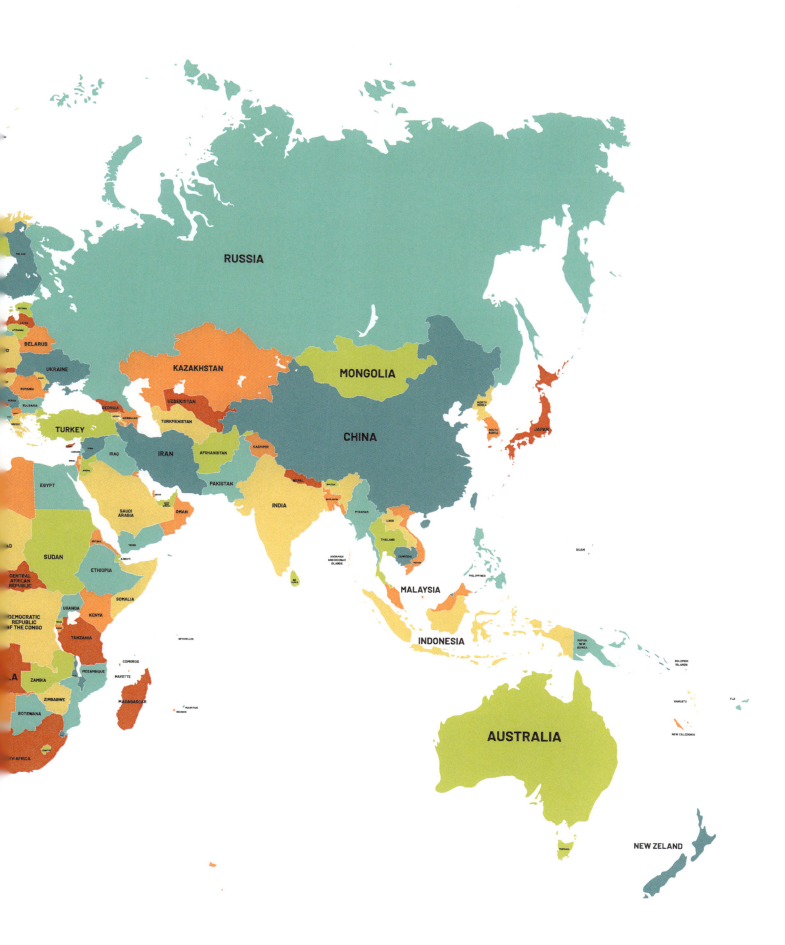

FLAGS OF THE USA

Alabama	Alaska	Arizona	Arkansas	California	Colorado	Connecticut
Delaware	Florida	Georgia	Hawaii	Idaho	Illinois	Indiana
Iowa	Kansas	Kentucky	Louisiana	Maine	Maryland	Massachusetts
Michigan	Minnesota	Mississippi	Missouri	Montana	Nebraska	Nevada
New Hampshire	New Jersey	New Mexico	New York	North Carolina	North Dakota	Ohio
Oklahoma	Oregon	Pennsylvania	Rhode Island	South Carolina	South Dakota	Tennessee
Texas	Utah	Vermont	Virginia	Washington	West Virginia	Wisconsin
Wyoming						

AMERICA

1. America has the largest economy in the world
2. Home to the best musical artist of all time
3. Home to Hollywood, the center of entertainment and one of the most famous places on Earth
4. Home to the Grand Canyon, one of the most popular tourist destinations
5. Home to Las Vegas, the entertainment capital of the world
6. The Missouri River is the 4th largest river in the world
7. Denali (Mt. McKinley), largest in North America is located in Alaska is 20,310 feet above sea level
8. Washington D.C. is the capital of the U.S.A.

I pledge allegiance

to the Flag

of the United States of America,

and to the Republic

for which it stands,

one Nation

under God,

indivisible,

with liberty

and justice for all,

INFLUENCERS

1. Father of the American Cartoon – Thomas Nast
2. Father of the Automobile – Karl Benz
3. Father of Biology – Aristotle
4. Father of Botany – Theophrastus
5. Father of Calculus – Gottfried Wilhelm Leibniz
6. Father of Computing – Charles Babbage
7. Father of Democracy – Cleisthenes, Greek
8. Father of Economics – Adam Smit
9. Father of Electricity – Michael Faraday
10. Father of English Language – Geoffrey Chaucer
11. Father of Genetics – Gregor Johann Mendel
12. Father of Geography – Eratosthenes
13. Father of History – Herodotus
14. Father of Idealism – Plato
15. Father of Impressionism – Claude Monet
16. Father of Invention – Thomas Alva Edison
17. Father of Mathematics – Archimedes
18. Father of Medicine – Hippocrates
19. Father of Modern Art – Paul Cézanne
20. Father of Modern Chess – Wilhelm Steinitz
21. Father of Modern Computer – Alan Turing
22. Father of Modern English Literature – William Shakespeare
23. Father of Modern Physics – Albert Einstein
24. Father of Modern Psychology – Sigmund Freud
25. Father of Modern Science – Galileo Galilei
26. Father of Nuclear Physics – Ernest Rutherford
27. Father of Photography – Nicéphore Niépce
28. Father of Physics – Galileo Galilei
29. Father of Printing – Johannes Gutenberg
30. Father of Psychology – Wilhelm Wundt
31. Father of the Renaissance – Petrarch
32. Father of the Scientific Method – Galileo Galilei
33. Father of Sociology – Auguste Comte
34. Father of Sports Psychology – Coleman Griffith
35. Father of Western Philosophy – Socrates
36. Father of Zoology – Aristotle

LANGUAGE

ENGLISH	ARABIC	FRENCH
Hello	as-salām 'alaykum or Salam!	bon-zhoor
Welcome! (to great someone)	Marhaban	
How are you?	kayfa ḥālik (f) / kayfa ḥālak (m)	kom-mohn tah-lay voo
I'm fine, and you?	Ana bikhair	bee-ehn mer-see ay voo?
My name is	... ismee	juh mah-pell
What is your name?	mā ismak/ik	kom-mohn voo-za-peh-lay voo
Please to meet you	motasharefatun bema'refatek (f) / motasharefon bema'refatek (m)	on-shohn-tay
Please	min fadlek	seel voo play
Thank you very much	shukran	Mehr-see boh-kuo
You're welcome	al'afw	duh ree-n
Excuse me (to pass by)	Alma'derah	ex-koo-zay mwah
Can You Help Me?	Hal beemkanek mosa'adati?	Poo-vey voo may-day?
Where is the ... ?	Ayna ajedu ... ?	oo es-keel ya ... ?
How Much Is This?	Kam howa thamanoh?	kel ey le pree?
Sorry	āsif!	zhuh swee day so lay
Yes/No	na'am / laa	wee / nohn
Goodbye	ma'a as-salāmah	oh ruh-vwar

ENGLISH	GERMAN	HINDI
Hello	goo-ten-taak	na-ma-ste
Welcome! (to great someone)		sva-gat
How are you?	Vee geht es see-nen?	āp kaise / kaisī hain? M/F
I'm fine, and you?	Goot, unt ee-nen?	main thik hun
My name is	ikh hai-se…	mira nam … hai
What is your name?	vee hai-sen zee?	tum-hara nam kya hai?
Please to meet you hui	ahn-ge-nehm / zair er-froyt	ap-se mil-kar ba-hut khushi
Please	bit-te	kri-pa-ya
Thank you	dahng-ke	shuk-riya
You're welcome	bit-te zair	ap-a-ka sva-gata hai
Excuse me (to pass by)	ent-SHOOL-de-gen zee	ksh-ama kee-jeeae
Can You Help Me?	ker-nen zee meer hell-fen?	tum-hem as-ir-va-da
Where is the … ?	vaw ist … ?	kyā āpa mērī madada karenge
How Much Is This?	vee feel kas-tet es?	ka-haang hay … ?
Sorry	ent-shul-di-gung	kit-ne kaa hay?
Yes/No	yaa / nian	han / nahin
Goodbye	owf vee-der zeh-en	na-ma-ste

ENGLISH	JAPANESE	RUSSIAN
Hello	ko-nee-chee-wa	pree-vee-et
Welcome! (to great someone)	yo-ko-so	doe-bro poh-za-loh-vat
How are you?	o gen-kee day-su ka	kak dee-la
I'm fine	o ka-ge-sa-ma de gen-ki day-su	hah-rah-sho
My name is	... da	mee-nyah zah-voot ...
What is your name?	o-nam-ae wa nan day-su ka?	kak vahs zah-voot?
Please to meet you	ha-jee-may-ma-shee-tay	pree-yaht-nah pahz-nah-koh-mee-tsah
Please	oh-ne-gai	pah-zhah-loo-shtah
Thank you	doe-moh ar-ee-ga-toe	spah-see-bah
You're welcome	do ee-tashi-ma-she-tay	pah-zhah-loo-shtah
Excuse me (to pass by)	shit-sur-ei shim-ass-oo	iz-vin-ee-te
Sorry	go-men na-sai	pra-stee-te
Can You Help Me?	Anata wa watashi o tasukeru koto ga dekimasu?	Vy mozhete mne pomoch?
Where is the ... ?	vaw ist ... ?	gde ... ?
How Much Is This?	vee feel kas-tet es?	skol-ka eta stoit?
Yes/No	hai / iie	dah / nyeet
Goodbye	sigh-ah-nar-ah	dah-svee-dah-nyah

ENGLISH	SPANISH	TURKISH
Hello	oh-luh	mer-ha-bah
Welcome! (to great someone)		hosh gel-din
How are you?	bee-en ven-ee-do	nah-sil-sin-ez?
I'm fine, and you?	co-mo est-as?	ee-yi-yim sa-ol, sin nah-sil-sin
My name is	bee-en	ad-im...
What is your name?	may yuhmoh ...	ad-in ne?
Please to meet you	koh-moh tay yuh-muh?	mem-nun old-um
Please	moo-choh goos-toh	lut-fen
Thank you very much	por fuh-vor	te-shek-kur ee-der-im
You're welcome	gra-si-as	bir shay day-eel
Excuse me (to pass by)	day na-duh	lut-fen
Can You Help Me?	me pwe-day a-yoo-dar-may	Bana yardım edebilir misiniz?
Where is the ... ?	don-de es-ta ... ?	neh-reh-deh ... ?
How Much Is This?	kwan-to kwes-ta?	neh kah-dahr?
Sorry	pair-doh-nah-may	ef-en-dim
Yes/No	see / non	ee-vet / hay-ear
Goodbye	uh-dee-os	goo-lay goo-lay

ASL - American Sign Language

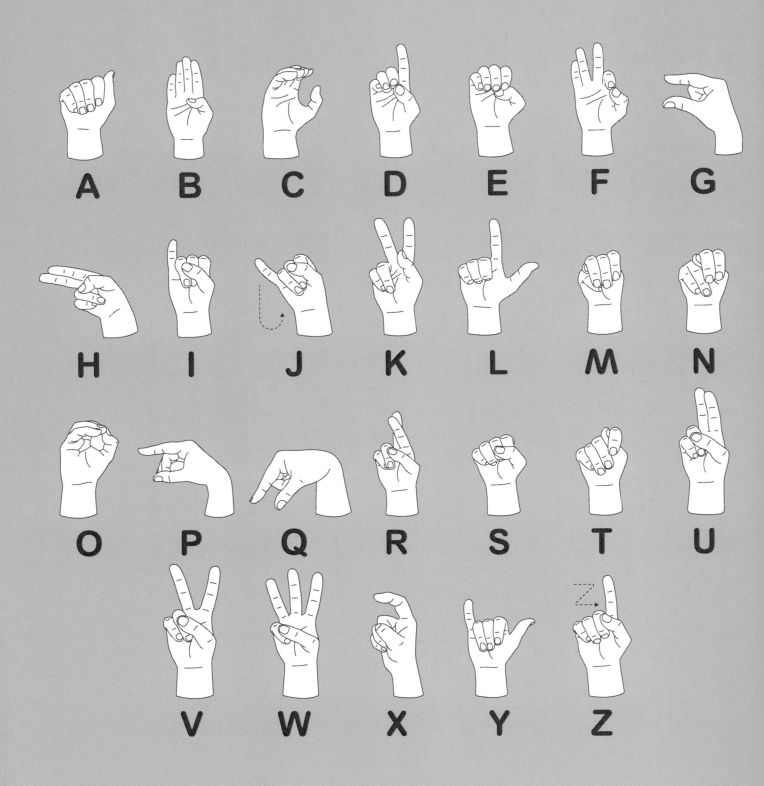

MEASUREMENT

1. 1 inch = 2.54 centimeters (cm)
2. 12 inches = 1 foot
3. 1 kilomenter (km) = .621 miles (mi)
4. Liberia, Myanmar and the United States are the only Countries that don't use the metric system
5. 1 mile (mi) = 5280 feet (ft)
6. 1 mile (mi) = 1.6 kilometer (km)

LENGTH

INCHES	DECIMAL	MM
1/16	0.06	1.59
1/8	0.13	3.18
3/16	0.19	4.76
1/4	0.25	6.35
5/16	0.31	7.94
3/8	0.38	9.53
7/16	0.44	11.11
1/2	0.50	12.70
9/16	0.56	14.29
5/8	0.63	15.88
11/16	0.69	17.46
3/4	0.75	19.05
13/16	0.81	20.64
7/8	0.88	22.23
15/16	0.94	23.81
1	1.00	25.40

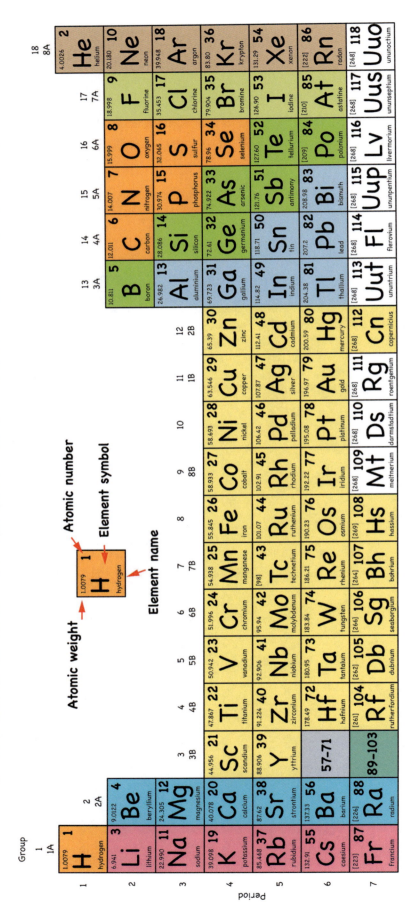

SCIENCE

Chemicals

1. Hydrogen, (H, #1) is the first element on the periodic table and is highly flammable gas
2. Helium, (He, #2) is lighter than air and is perfect for balloons because it helps them float
3. Lithium, (Li, #3) soft enough to cut with a knife, floats on water, does not occur naturally
4. Beryllium, (Be, #4) used in alloys w/ copper/nickel to make gyroscopes, springs & electrical contacts
5. Boron, (B, #5) is used for building strong bones but should be taken in very small doeses
6. Carbon, (C, #6) comes in different forms to include diamond, graphite and impure forms like coal
7. Nitrogen, (N, #7) makes up about 78% of the air you breathe and is in all living things
8. Oxygen, (O, #8) is very reactive that easily forms compounds such as oxides. 21% of air you breathe
9. Fluorine, (F, #9) used to make plastics, such as Teflon, and also important in dental health
10. Neon, (Ne, 10) used in plasma, television, vacuum, and wave meter tubes,
11. Sodium, (Na, #11)
12. Magnesium, (Mg, #12)
13. Aluminum, (Al, #13)
14. Silicon, (Si, #14)
15. Phosphorous (P, #15) is the oldest chemical element
16. Sulfer, (S, #16) is yellow and one of the top 8 most abundant elements in the human body
17. Chlorine, (Cl, #17) 3rd most abundant element in the oceans
18. Potassium, (K, #19)
19. Calcium, (Ca, #20)
20. Titanium, (Ti, #22)
21. Iron, (Fe, #26)
22. Nickel, (Ni, #28)
23. Copper, (Cu, #29)
24. Zinc, (Zn, #30)
25. Arsenic, (As, #33)
26. Krypton, (Kr, #36)
27. Silver, (Ag, #47)
28. Cadmium, (Cd, #48)
29. Tin, (Sn, #50)
30. Iodine, (I, #53)
31. Gold, (Au, #79)
32. Mercury, (Hg, #80)
33. Astatine, (At, #85) is the rarest naturally occurring element on Earth's crust
34. Uranium, (U, #92)
35. Plutonium, (Pu, #94) is the most dangerous, radioactive, toxic elements in the world
36. Einsteinium, (Es, #99)
37. Mendelevium, (Md, #101)
38. Hassium (Hs, #108) is the newest chemical element
39. Veritasium, The element of Truth. ☺

Branches of Science
1. An Astronomer is a scientist who studies outer space
2. A Biologist is a scientist who studies life
3. A Botonist is a scientist who studies plants
4. A Chemist is a scientist who studies atomic matter
5. A Cosmologist is a scientist who studies rocks
6. A Entomologist is a scientist who studies insects
7. A Geologist is a scientist who studies rocks
8. A Hydrologist is a scientist who studies water
9. A Marine Biologist is a scientist who studies ocean animals and plants
10. A Meteorologist is a scientist who studies weather
11. A Oncologist is a scientist who studies cancer
12. A Physicist is a scientist who studies energy and matter
13. A Psychologist is a scientist who studies human behavior
14. A Zoologist is a scientist who studies Animals

Greatest Scientists
1. Galileo Galilei is the father of modern science because of his discoveries in astronomy and physics
2. Nikola Tesla known for designing the (AC) electric system, the 'Tesla coil' used in radio technology
3. Albert Einstein developed general theory of relativity $E=mc^2$ on which the atomic bomb is based
4. Sir Isaac Newton was known for his law on gravitation, invented calculus, reflecting telescope
5. Louis Pasteur explained the 'Germ Theory', created 'Pasteurization' a process treating milk
6. Marie Curie Sklodowska is the first female to be awarded with a Nobel Prize
7. Thomas Alva Edison patented 1093 inventions, include batteries, cement, lights, phonographs
8. Michael Faraday discovered benzene, principles of electromagnetic, diamagnetism, & electrolysis
9. Archimedes is regarded as the greatest mathematician of all time
10. Aristotle was a biologist, ethicist, zoologist, a political scientist, a master of rhetoric and logic

Water

1. Water is called H2O because it has 2 Hydrogen atoms and 1 Oxygen
2. 68.7% of the fresh water on Earth is trapped in glaciers
3. 30% of fresh water is in the ground
4. Approximately 400 billion gallons of water are used in a day in the USA
5. The average residence uses over 100,000 gallons of water (indoors and outside)
6. Water can dissolve more substances than any other liquid including sulfuric acid
7. About 6,800 gallons of water is required to grow a day's food for a family of four
8. One pint of beer takes 20 gallons of water to create
9. 780 million people lack access to an improved water source
10. 200 million work hours are consumed by women to collect water for their families each day
11. 200 children die an hour from unsafe water
12. Water weighs about 8 pounds a gallon
13. 70% of the human brain is water

SOLAR SYSTEM

Heat, Hottest & Temperature

1. Sun is 27 million degrees Fahrenheit (15 million degrees Celsius)
2. Venus is 880°F (471°C)
3. Furnace Creek Ranch in Death Valley, CA reached 134°F Hottest recorded temperature on Earth
4. Dragon's Breath chili pepper is world's hottest. Eat and can cause anaphylactic shock and kill you

WORLD RECORDS

Largest
1. Largest animal is the blue whale
2. Largest Bungy jump is Bloukrans Bridge Bungy 709 feet
3. Largest country in the world is Russia
4. Largest desert is the Sahara
5. Largest economy in the world is the U.S.A.
6. Largest flower is the Rafflesia (meter across) found in Indonesia, Malaysia, and Thailand
7. Largest living structure on Earth is The Great Barrier Reef off Australian Coast
8. Largest planet in our solar system is Jupiter
9. Largest river is the Nile

Shortest & Smallest
1. World's shortest people in the world come from Indonesia
2. World's smallest mammal is the Kitti's hog-nosed bat aka bumblebee bat located in Burma

Our Father which art in heaven,

Hallowed be thy name.

Thy kingdom come,

Thy will be done in earth,

as it is in heaven.

Give us this day our daily bread.

And forgive us our debts,

as we forgive our debtors.

And lead us not into temptation,

but deliver us from evil:

For thine is the kingdom,

and the power, and the glory,

forever. Amen.

Baltimore

1. 1st Umbrella factory in the United States was established in 1828
2. 1st United States post office system was inaugurated in 1774
3. 1st dental school in the world was founded in 1840
4. 1st telegraph line in the world was established between Washington, D.C. and Baltimore in 1844
5. 1st civic monument of President George Washington, Baltimore's Washington Monument.
6. 1st successful manned balloon launch in USA operated by Edward Warren in 1784
7. 1st professional sports organization in the USA, The Maryland Jockey Club formed in 1743
8. 1st Catholic cathedral built in USA is Baltimore Basilica of Assumption
9. 1st to illuminate streetlamps with hydrogen gas in 1816
10. 1st bloodshed of the Civil War, a clash between pro-South civilians and Union troops in 1861
11. 1st black-owned shipyard in the USA.
12. 1st to make Snowballs, which paved way for modern slushies and snow cones
13. BWI airport is the 1st and only US airport to have a dedicated trail for hiking and biking
14. Francis Scott Key wrote National Anthem watching Fort McHenry bombardment in War of 1812
15. Michael Phelps is the most decorated Olympian of all time with 22 medals
16. Babe Ruth, Cal Ripken, Jr. Billy Ripken, Lefty Grove, and many more were born in Baltimore
17. Edgar Allan Poe died in Baltimore, and was buried at Westminster Hall and Burial Grounds
18. Thurgood Marshall, the first African American Supreme Court Justice was born in 1908
19. Reginal F. Lewis, the first African American to own a billion-dollar company honored with museum
20. Billie Holiday, the late great world-famous jazz singer has a monument in her honor
21. Julie Bowen, Jada Pinkett Smith, Mike Rowe, Montel Williams born in Baltimore
22. Famous people who lived in Baltimore include Cab Calloway, 2Pac, Oprah Winfrey

Maryland

1. Tori Amos moved to Baltimore and grew up in Rockville and Silver Spring
2. Toni Braxton, born in Severn, MD, attended Bowie State University
3. Kathie Lee Gifford, raised in Bowie, Md, attended Bowie H.S.
4. Goldie Hawn, raised in Takoma Park, MD, attended Montgomer Blair H.S.
5. Joan Jett was raised in Rockville and attended Randolph J.H. and Wheaton H.S.
6. Martin Lawrence, attended high school in Landover and Fort Washington
7. Julia Louis-Drewfus, graduated from Holton-Arms School in Bethesda, MD
8. William H. Macy, grew up in Cumberland, went to Allegany H.S.
9. Edward Norton, Columbia, MD

10 Things About Me ☺

1. Name (What name means) _____

2. Born _____

3. Favorite Book(s) _____

4. Favorite Movie(s) _____

5. Favorite Music _____

6. Favorite Quote _____

7. Favorite Show _____

8. I want to be _____

9. I want to meet _____

10. I Love _____

About Kenny

Kenny 'K3' Rochon, III is a 7-year-old boy, Game Changer - Leader. He recently was published as an author, and he is an expert in children's jokes.

When K3 is not telling jokes, he is playing chess with his daddy, learning how to code, playing Minecraft and Nintendo, and even some learning games that challenge his inquisitive and problem-solving mind.

He enjoys math, playing Sudoku, and expanding his vocabulary with his "Kenny's Fortune" word box. Kenny's Future Word Box is a future product he is coming out with the help other children learn the military alphabet and learn positive powerful words. He uses these words to hone up on his skills as a proficient speller so he can win spelling bees.

He has a yellow belt in Tae Kwon Do and practices so he can protect his Mommy (and Daddy) from danger.

Drawing by Stephania Christianson

About Ken Rochon

Ken loves his son Kenny. He enjoys writing a new book every year to celebrate his son's life and to share valuable lessons with him on character, leadership, and success

You can listen to Ken on his radio show Amplified with Ken Rochon, through the VoiceAmerica Influencer Channel on Mondays at 11 AM Eastern, on Itunes or at www.AmplifiedRadioShow.com

This is Ken's 28th book and now his favorite :) He wants to inspire other parents to create a legacy of love with their children through publishing. Ken has created templates that make publishing books more effortless and affordable. (www.PerfectPublishing.com)

Besides playing with his son, Ken loves to travel the world and has been to over 100 countries. He is a world class photographer and enjoys covering the biggest events in the USA (www.BIGeventsUSA.com)

If you are interested in having Ken speak at your school or event, simply connect with him on Facebook or email him at Ken@TheUmbrellaSyndicate.com.

Ken is the co-founder of the Keep Smiling Movement.com. He has co-authored a series of books focused on setting your mindset to be positive. Check out on Amazon the *Keep Smiling – Shift Happens* Series.

He resides in the Baltimore Washington Metropolitan Area with his family.

More of Kenny's Books

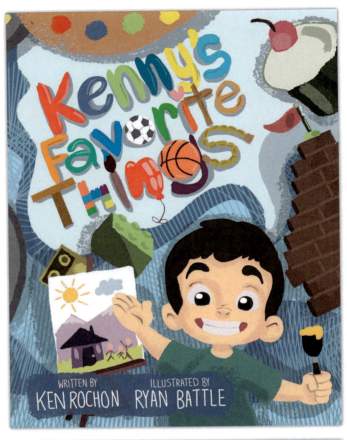
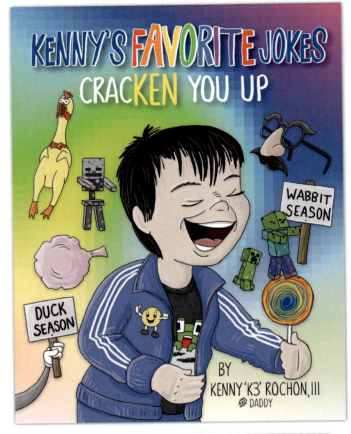
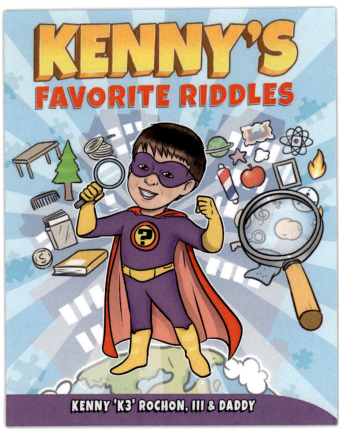
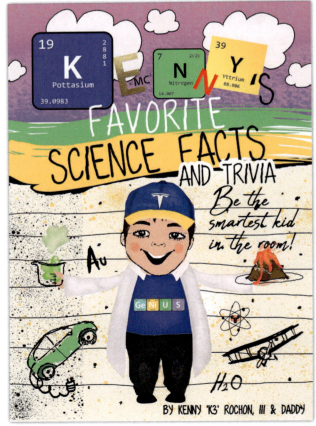

More of Kenny's Books

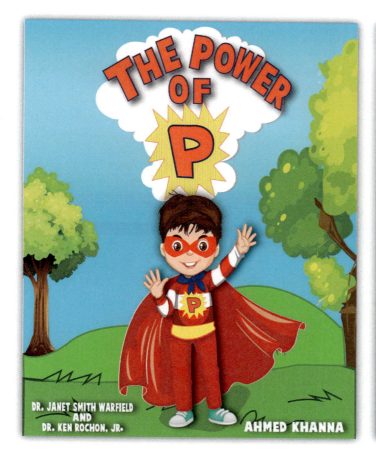
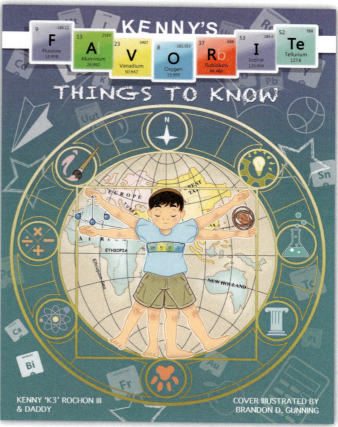
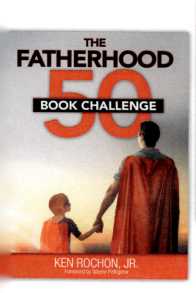
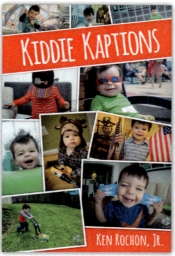
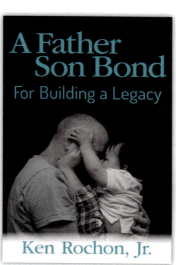
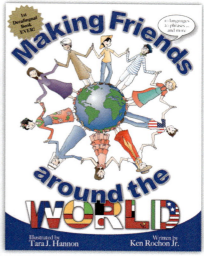